D1499623

Marrow

Marrow

POEMS

darlene anita scott

 UNIVERSITY PRESS OF KENTUCKY

Scholarly publisher for the Commonwealth, serving Bellarmine University, Berea College, Centre College of Kentucky, Eastern Kentucky University, The Filson Historical Society, Georgetown College, Kentucky Historical Society, Kentucky State University, Morehead State University, Murray State University, Northern Kentucky University, Spalding University, Transylvania University, University of Kentucky, University of Louisville, and Western Kentucky University. All rights reserved.

Editorial and Sales Offices: The University Press of Kentucky
663 South Limestone Street, Lexington, Kentucky 40508-4008
www.kentuckypress.com

Library of Congress Cataloging-in-Publication Data

Names: scott, darlene anita, author.
Title: Marrow : poems / darlene anita scott.
Description: Lexington, Kentucky : The University Press of Kentucky, [2022]
 | Series: University Press of Kentucky new poetry and prose
Identifiers: LCCN 2021042927 | ISBN 9780813183619 (hardcover ; acid-free
 paper) | ISBN 9780813183626 (paperback ; acid-free paper) | ISBN
 9780813183633 (pdf) | ISBN 9780813183640 (epub)
Subjects: LCGFT: Poetry.
Classification: LCC PS3619.C66145 M37 2022 | DDC 811/.6—dc23/eng/20211006
LC record available at https://lccn.loc.gov/2021042927

Member of the Association of University Presses

ASSOCIATION
of UNIVERSITY
PRESSES

For the children of Peoples Temple

Contents

PART 4

Marrow

Part 1

In 1954 James "Jim" Jones first established Peoples Temple as the Community Unity Church in his hometown, Indianapolis. In 1955 the church became Wings of Deliverance and in 1956 Peoples Temple. In 1960 the church became an affiliate of the Disciples of Christ denomination.

Each iteration of the church was a racial mix reflecting Jones's commitment to racial and class equality. In 1965 the church moved to California, where members began to practice a communal lifestyle that included foster children who were given the opportunity to rehabilitate there instead of in detention facilities.

The congregation was a social force in California politics that attracted young, upper-middle-class, progressive whites to its largely African American and working-class membership as well as others who were disenchanted by traditional Christianity.

Shelby County, Alabama
1917

Center of the state; moonshiningest county in it.
Coordinates or crosshairs. There's always more than one way
to look a thing in the eye. Even a white man. Always suh or ma'am.
Insults & compliments, the same: affirmative.
Covered in my shadow: Can I he-lp you [darkie].
Be a faithful & diligent darkie: eat your food &
go to church darkie. Dusting powder & Christmas
whiskey. Dilute with water & just don't sing over the choir.
The porter's boy & Baker's Grove Baptist. Cotton & camelia.
Route 70 & the blackberries. Sun wring a relief in sweat: gentle
as my lover's finger tiptoeing this timber of spine.

The Invitation
29 April 1960

Sun molests colored glass
converts sidewalk to fresco.

We are rumored contagion—
even the landscape submits.

Pilgrims come to suckle
its spell: *I will have you*
   if you let me.

To All to Whom These Presents Shall Come, Greeting
17 February 1965

>*[ARTICLE VII]:*
>*If the memberships are to be divided into classes*
>*the designations of the different classes,*
>*and a statement of the relative rights,*
>*preferences, limitations and restrictions*
>*of each class, together with a statement*
>*as to the voting rights of any such class:*
>*No Division into classes present.*

Bring
     your bodies
     your burdens.
Rest
     your labors
     your wraps.
     Come!
Be blessed
& a blessing.

Rostrum

3 August 1965

You leave my body many times before I stop counting.

                    In relief first.

Disappointment then
with the same anger
You pummel into my stomach.

                    I absorb You to saturation.

Buckle into burlap
tuck in a cargo hold

                    until the scent of You
                    is too stale to recognize.

            *

                    until the scent of You
                    is too stale to recognize.

                    I absorb You to saturation.

                    In relief first.

You leave my body many times before I stop counting.

            *

tuck in a cargo hold
Buckle into burlap

You pummel into my stomach.
with the same anger
Disappointment then

You leave my body many times before I stop counting.

※

You leave my body many times before I stop counting.

Disappointment then
with the same anger
You pummel into my stomach.

Buckle into burlap
tuck in a cargo hold

                    In relief first.

                    I absorb You to saturation.

                    until the scent of You
                    is too stale to recognize.

※

Bookish Girl Sweeps the Sanctuary

5 September 1970

> *If you find yourself in boredom to such a degree it*
> *is difficult to contemplate on esoteric values, it is*
> *not something to be discouraged about necessarily.*
> *It can be a sign that the detachment you have been*
> *working for has come.*
>
> *Pastor Jim*
> PEOPLES TEMPLE FLYER

In the Acts: all that believed
were together & had all things
in common. In my bag, apples
the size of my fist bump & bruise.

I chase dry my petition for a sober
whose blooming does not chafe,
Prell that convinces boys & bounce.
Bay my selfish prattle with chore.

Coax from the broom's hiss a rhythmic
flagellation: there| arehard| erplaces| tobe.

The Black Book

30 June 1972

*Eleven o'clock on Sunday morning is one of the
most segregated hours, if not the most segregated
hour[s], in Christian America.*

  Martin Luther King Jr.
  MEET THE PRESS

Once I believed a white version
of murky pictures verging sheer.
The sea of men & women & crops,
all of them crops, flagging in the
sepia scape like so many stars.

You choose, instead, a Bible to crease
their backs; dissolve them with the
venom of your spit because after all,
stars are heedless fires & must be
extinguished or harnessed for use.

The dirge & dank of it fills the sanctuary,
awkward as imminent death can be.
This gospel will eventually claim us all
except me, you decree, proud prodigal
cavorting & integrating into that sea.

A Revolutionary Love Story
5 October 1972

> *I want to be in on changing the world to be a better*
> *place and I would give my life for it.*
> *Annie Moore*

We step bravely into the fasting.
Salty skinned & doe eyed;
more got than give. The wild,
ferrous & mossy, thickens
our hair, intoxicates us holy.

We might crave God's good earth
when it's not the bowl of our backs
turned on their faces, empty. Might be
sincere in our giddy abstinence ripe
with the way God makes. Except the one.

He doesn't. I draw a circle in your palm;
bullseye it with my pointer: We are Here.
Then slurp. You only jerk away to be coy.
You're intoxicated by the smell of my hair
dusting your calluses in its own drizzle of kisses.

Water

7 April 1975

I.

We end each night as it shrinks from night
by making love; charm each day like a snake

from its urn. Toward becoming we float damp
as molting; deliciously cautious in the dew

of young skin's patience & pliancy. Bellying every
stone unloved by water: our car toting a gallon

in the back seat in case the engine changes its mind
midway. Sharing what we don't have with passengers.

Odetta out of tune for the sojourn: No matter
who *says no, I'll go alone. I'm on my way, great God!*

May children bloom in the wet of our works; may these works,
our pour of water, gray us in official photos, disappear us into our faith.

II.

She says we wear our dungarees mighty tight, walk taller
than the doorsill, demand too much of our bed springs. She

leaves white cotton slips & fig preserves at the end of summer,
refuses the baby's bag: she's been here longer than we've been

smelling ourselves. Rocks him against the sweet spot between
her chin & clavicle; a blade concealed in the dried tobacco leaves

that assimilate her breasts. Said she came from tobacco-picking people.
Come with Vaseline to keep babies' cheeks & after-nap knees shiny

as new nickels; with quilts, baby-girl totems for pixie eyes
to flutter to seal; thumbs limp, loose & spitty at their lips.

Come with pennies to press & preserve mama spirit
in fresh belly buttons. Come to ombre her brown

to grey in the official photo that disappears her
into her faith. Come to be useful.

Wild Child

17 March 1976

I claimed sidewalks,
smeared the cracks under the balls of my feet,
culled a cadence for boys with my gum. Hungry & wild
until a good feeding, my name called like a consecration.
All it took to cross my body its allegiances, balm scabs to scars,
shave to shameless prickly, lop to tufts Larry, Dave, Carroll, flurry
of snowflakes melting as soon as they landed at my planted feet.

Jubilee

23 May 1976

I.
open clip open clap ... clip ... clap
knees fan for heat, invitation
for the initiated; annoyance
to the pew dwellers rocking
to my rhythm. Their own
would otherwise be a shuffling
waltz of 1s taking their time to 2s.

II.
Sitting still is stupid the boy swings
Buster Browns, mallets to the bottom
of the bench, nearly kicking the rear
of the lady in front. Except his legs
are too short. He practices plusses
& take-aways. Ladies whimper & sway.
Men brine in their sweat. Pastor heaves, shrieks,
Shit. There is more, but his hangnail stings. He
bites & sucks the blood under the shifted skin;
attention sets on the burgundy polyester of a
pant leg, bell of it ringing in its private breeze.

III.
I nod from sleeplessness
only I know. Drive-thru reels
fidgeting soundless: my folks.
Good & faithful servant
pretending to heat like moon

shine: slow scorch of flaming
wool. To hunger bright & tipsy
stumbling into the walls of my belly.

IV.
I picked something pretty.
You have to pull it tight
behind both ears.
Tie a knot
to keep it in place.
Then wrap. Tuck
where you must.
Wait until you've
wrapped & tucked
all of the fabric
to look in the mirror
& adjust accordingly.

Part 2

The land that would become Jonestown, the Peoples Temple Agricultural Project, was leased to Peoples Temple in 1974. The purchased land was on the disputed border between Venezuela and Guyana, which would presumably protect the Guyanese from military action. It was under a triple canopy, the thickest jungle in which any vegetation can grow. Additionally, the country was relatively poor, having just gained independence from Britain, and, though mostly indigenous, the Guyanese were English speaking. These factors contributed to the attractiveness of the acquisition and the ease with which Jones secured it.

When several members defected and contributed to a media exposé, Jim Jones decided to move where the congregation could exist without scrutiny. In the summer of 1977, the mass exodus from Peoples Temple's California headquarters to Guyana began.

The Peoples Temple Agricultural Project
23 April 1974

Earth is a mama
who plies patience,
unafraid of denying.
Trains her wisdom
on the devil of details.
Her tipping point
is shifty weight,
liquid volume.

Wishing Tree

6 June 1977

His hair needles my thigh; strokes
bright like citrus; conflagration of

scarlet, saffron, lemon, vermilion.
I grab a handful. Tidy our want

to order: Mama, welfare lady,
doubt mute between my fingers.

He's fine. And when he says
we're going to be, I believe.

I braid; he slicks in & out
of promises tendered for nights

he can't get home. Coated in wounds
& funk so we eat good, make love good—

Baby, he says, *we found it.* The garden
lingers on his breath; his hands totem

my belly like a wishing tree
so he can believe too.

For Yonder

Summer 1977

Q-tips
~~candy~~
Cruex
lotion
peroxide
~~passport~~
Desenex
Vaseline
hair comb
toothpaste
3 kerchiefs
toothbrush
witch hazel
baking soda
body powder
12 boxes Kotex

field hat
2 pr jeans
1 pr slacks
5 tee shirts
rubber boots
5 underwear
2 pr jean shorts
5 pr underwear
24 pr tube socks
1 pr thick thongs
1 button-up shirt
1 pr tennis shoes

my tapes
tape player
*get TiTi's address
sleeping bag/blanket
toilet paper (seal in plastic)
No *exceptances* will be made.

Composting

30 July 1977

The soil did not swaddle;
would not entertain
in careless adoration
demands we made of it:
stripping, caressing, coaxing.
Until we learned how to cow.

Held the press of our weight
tighter than promises.
So we saturated it
with accelerants like wonder
& hunger. Warmed it with
our hopeful & certain bodies.

Making Soap
13 August 1977

Sweat forms a gracious caul over us, hovering & humming:

> *Do not let the lye touch your skin.*

Blessed babies gather in its bag of waters until the very moment
they enter this plane. Saved & placed under the bed of the dying,
it lubricates the channels back. Sweat is the best we can do
in our sorcery of lard & ash.

> *Avoid inhaling fumes, ventilate.*
> *Cover your eyes. Mix vigorously.*

Egyptians recorded as remedy & protection what we regard as hygiene.
Like babies & the dying traversing the same plane, different directions.
Invention is a kind of lie we are gifted. God is a chance we take. After all,
frontier women, too, hovered over cauldrons creasing their hands, yet
plague.

Disappearance

19 August 1977

for James S. Baisy Sr.

Daddies are more than conduit
hemming need to desire.
Daddies disappear women, replace
them with automata plump & righteous
sprouting supplementary limbs;
lenses that see behind the head &
around the corner long before fast
legs sprint sugar fortified to some
delicious danger. Call them mamas.

Mamas don't wait. Hover, hum & strike.
Daddies seep into searches after
their shifts. Become men disappeared:
distorted stain of sweat on the sofa,
cushion rimless like molten lava heaving.
The wells of their throats dilate to bellies;
marrow replaced with the slurp of
still-learning-language babies summoning
them: *Daddy.*

The Rules

5 September 1977

No excessive talking. Verb silence & manage your tongue like crushed glass. Let your words leak into your gums no less than if they were embedded in your soles, multiplying sharpness under your weight. Do not call names, hit (even playfully), mishandle property, enter the brush for any reason. Stay within sight. Trust your skin's caution against barb & venom. Deceit has its uses: in nature bright colors attract to alarm poison; your breath with its false prophecy of control. Refrain from negativism, complaining, extreme cursing, showing disrespect. No returning late from breaks. Practice modesty in all things; abstinence from all habit-forming substances & the temptation of worldly gains & material good/s.

How Today Will Look When It's History

14 September 1977

Two days ago I turned 28. Steven Biko was deaded in South Africa. Two days before he was 30, proud canon, fire & song. Two days later he is 30, proud canon, fire & song. Two days later twin plaits on either side of my head announce themselves despite my scarf, wed once & then again for cause: rainstorm, an incantation I inhale with the brine & tallow scent of Band-Aids, craft tongue depressors into trinkets for the children, imagine my lover's ankles announcing themselves from the cuffs of her clam diggers. I have fallen in love twice. Damon filled me with his witless plans; said in the house, we *shared too much to ever give an honest damn about anyone,* only everyone. When he escaped, I did too. A quarter page scribbled between us; eventually, the tenuous measure of more language plus sea. My new lover fills me with rice. There is usually rice. I consume it as affidavit to my deading. Today I am 28. A rainstorm is in duet with the quotidian. Storms come nearly every day, canon & song.

I Learn to Love the Body She Loves
28 September 1977

My fix blows,   to pretty; sparkle cloud.
                        pixie dust without a fairytale,
            All   these neurons
                                                    buzzing

            so orderly the hum is its own
            silence. I am high   as a kite

            my papa would say. Said too,

*the devil you know is
better than the one you don't.*

I take two: eucharist of pixie dust & my favorite psalm

scenting the shower earthen.
She holds my hand in public &

lets me finger the thick scar
tumbling
            jagged
                into the
                        ravine   of
                                    her
                                    crack.

A Tree Gets in the Way
11 November 1977

Loudspeakers lullaby
in their frequency
The microphone lobs
each of its disasters like
so much phlegm
in a raucous wind
rebellious chromatics
squawking a test pattern
to confirm: there is no god.
Savior between earth & sky,
a tree absorbs each shadow
with the tithes of our grateful light.

The Twenty-Fifth
23 December 1977

> *We're making a lot of game boards and manipulative materials (blocks, puzzles) that will eventually be marketed throughout Guyana besides our toys.*
> *Pat Grunnet, to her mother*

Sanding is spiritual work.
Hands, the main organ

by which to manipulate
the environment, polish.

Everything deserves
the attention of sheen.

We were splintery;
jagged intention.

In satisfied squeaks, rag to wood,
we mind to extract the same

from boys & girls
fidgety & impatient.

Their fingertips, massive clumps
of nerves capable of feeling almost

better than any other part
of the human body,

will fondle us with
the carelessness of their age.

God's vanity abides
this life's work of play.

Christine
5 January 1978

has never had a man
make her feel certain
and willing to take to
careless in the absence
of her jewelry never been
that naked or green as
the time between hard and tender
was always an exchange sharp as
the machete in his hands clearing her
way through the only kind of heaven
she recognizes: overbearingly lush,
accessible by force, prying it
open sweating into the
damp of it. A raspy
secret sits on her
finger, a ring
violating
his spell.

Bucket Brigade
6 March 1978

The aluminum passes from
hand to hand in automation.
Stretching skin threadbare
over biceps, rheumatic will
& digits. Sun extracts salt &
feeds the bodies' water to
plants like milk's command
to maturity. Boiled, fried, or
mashed they serve their vic-
tories at each night's dinner.

Harvesting

1 April 1978

Our hands dodge mischievous monkeys
& mosquitoes to coax poison to vaccine.
Toxic when raw, itchy if undercooked,
brings malaria, dengue & yellow fever
to yield its colorful costume: *sweet, nutty*
flavor when boiled or mashed or stewed.

Cassava is a root we excavate again & again.
We buried Lela Murphy too close to our
water supply. This, of course, is unsafe
as raw cassava. Dead bodies leak; bring
diarrheal illness. Reverend Edwards dug
her up, reburied her to preserve us like
cassava.

How Sleep Finds Us

8 April 1978

> *Get up at seven and be out there, if you care*
> *about the liberation of our people.*
>
> Community Meeting
> TAPE Q597

If it can, as disruption. An accusation.
Dense catalog, precise measure, or
escape: thick, impassable darkness

complicit & tight-lipped to the day's
transgressions. As punishment; weapon.
Clammy. And never a casual puzzle.

For now, our dreams are indulgence
best left with haints & tricksters.
Take the sleep. Take only the sleep.

Don't be duped: the satisfaction of sleep
is fleeting as the verve just before love
making ends. Postcoital rigor mortis.

Maybe the gratification to which we return
like we do to sleep: transfer of labor & reward.

Sometimes Molasses
17 April 1978

Nights when the stars cloak themselves like taut virgins

Nights the tangle of bamboo are old men's knees clapping &

would twist limbs into a soft, chewed alphabet of bumbling

& misuse. Nights thick as molasses. Damp blanket of heat

dark & elusive as molasses. Nights that shatter under anvils

of desire, evaporate into the woodsy scent of his penis; tart

requiem of their sex. Nights called by proper names: Monday,

Thursday, Tuesday. Waning in twilight bloating into weeks:

ravaged afternoons left for birds to pluck & collect for breakfast.

Government Name
25 May 1978

Hiss of ripped paper & an old woman's cackle
are bedsprings that trace & announce
the length of the girl. Talons declawed
by an honest day's damn end, her arm
slung over the bunk, in sleep reaching
for a beyond without red lights.

She was meant to move her weight;
noisy her name & not apologize for it.
One hundred times a day & twice before
bed keeps the teeth in her mouth straight;
her toes in front of her heels:

my name needs no noise;
choruses are better than a single note.

my name needs no noise;
choruses are better than a single note.

Her mama said she was the color of
coconut flesh, dingy white. A question.
So her mama calls her the old way.
Chalky on her tongue; a challenge her
daughter will not survive: *my name*
needs no noise; choruses are better
than a single note.

What We Talk About in Our Cottage

13 June 1978

Whether to order beans or wheat.
If all else fails.
Because we can't live without it.
Athlete's foot.
Crazy, laughable & common,
Cover of make-believe
(managing absolutes clumsily).

When Shanda Said No

29 July 1978

Angels were tired of minding their harps
So they sat down & plucked a chromatic strum Just one strum
The earth did not tilt   Boys in Adidas poured their legs
into cutoffs   They loped the periphery stalking opportunities
for mayhem   No babies were born   The sun was heavy-handed
No one shrank from its caress   Elders swayed & sweat on porches
Flies made merry in the latrines the Learning Crew dashed about
their breath supplication to breeze   An 11 year old chewed
the drawstring of her shirt   A transistor spit, gurgled, wheezed
some news   Some music might have happened   Someone
was probably peeing   Yeast & salt sweetened the air   A napping baby
might have sneezed   A cornrow was unraveling

The Scent of Her Grooming

20 September 1978

of swollen wood planks;
wetness a mingle of moss, straw & hops.
of damp clay; of many, chatting in wait.
Of she, yawning thick breath, drawing
lines in the mud with steady eyes, lips
full in repose; stones over the tomb
where urge & gumption have retreated.

Brick of lye soap after two days
a latherless sliver of decided cleanliness.
There is lotion. Of unfamiliar flora;
crumbling white buds of antiperspirant
flowering under her arms—wheat field
in sunlight downy, then, along her forearms.

Of the day's aria; macaws & hoes attacking
acres of lazy faith for a good day of rice, gravy,
bananas. For a good day of rice, gravy,
bananas. For a good day of rice, gravy,
bananas. Rice, gravy, bananas. Gravy, rice,
bananas. Gravy. Rice. Bananas.

In Defense of Devotion

6 October 1978

My sole purpose in recording
this is so you all may know.

The only reason I'm doing it
is to tell you all the Truth.

Eyes don't speak;
mouths can't hear.

So much has been said that is not
the Truth, and you should know
What Really Happened.

Hypotheses are where
experiments mislead.

I tell you this to make it clear.
Because I am tired of the Lies.

This is what happened.
Everything here is true.

Part 3

In 1973, the Peoples Temple Choir recorded the album *He's Able*. The opening song, "Welcome," is performed by the Peoples Temple's junior choir, comprised of members between five and twelve years old:

Although the days may be drear, He always is near,
And that's why my heart is always filled with song;
I'm singing, singing, all day long.

In just over five years after the recording, all of the young performers would be dead.

Spit Shine

20 March 1966

Think patent leather, Easter Sunday, or homecoming:
even the scratches shone. Think the heel of Mama's hands
kneading Vaseline & lotion down your cheeks; thumbing
its ash-seeking moisture into the corners of your eyes. Think
near-gossamer socks rolled to ruffles. Think twist puff to root,
barrettes smelling like sleep & stale Blue Magic. Not Easter
or homecoming or a social worker's visit; important the same.
Think the stir & tittering over your company a riddle; so many
hands like clammy biscuit dough passing your body along the pew;
in cadence with the clapping choir, robes in sway; clipped & intoned
consonants pouring faith in your mama's ears from a white man's
dispense, a curiosity. Think about separating your closed eyes;
slow then blink. Think about collapsing the furrow between
your brows. Think the smell of her sweat-diluted perfume
& uncover a sneeze.

Algebra
25 January 1974

Only one boy. Whose teeth
task the boundaries of his lips.
Raises his hand to solve for x.
But is not selected. He is a boy
without a Father. Is the Boy
who plots Russia on the globe;
has memorized the sickle of her
coordinates intersecting like x;
like the eggs he misses as much
as any boy deserves eggs.

He rewrites his homework
after detangling hostile knots of
ill-assorted letters & numbers:
reluctant but necessary unraveling.
Bubbles of 5s swell to orbs
curved aloof as undisturbed
egg shells. When x is stubborn
to disentangle, fissure along the
curve of his not-yet-useful pubis
oozes like viscous albumen,
like a Father in reluctant unraveling,
to waterlog his incubating ambitions.

Makeshift Daddy
22 October 1976

I use my full foot; roll heel then toe.
My body convicts my ma's friends.
At night they beg forgiveness
cloaked in grateful tears.

School comes to me a cadence.
Script precise & sure.

Fear & ego fail me.
I will write screenplays,
get the girl, hang from the rim
refusing to move from recollection.

The baby girl gods me.
I lob my voice like fertilizer;
shush my brothers
until their turn comes.

Every afternoon glistening with
the victory of my limbs

flexed in the tilling of heat
for a sooner harvest.

For Just Pennies a Glass
24 October 1977

*Flavor Aid turns an ordinary pitcher of water into
a delicious fruity drink for just pennies a glass!
Flavor Aid comes in thirteen refreshing flavors!*
    Jel Sert website

Cherry.
      Dregs memories of sidewalks
      chalked & too hot to walk barefoot.
      Moustaches stained above
      Mickey Mouse mics, squeaking
      to a reach beyond their years.
      Anyway, children are half kinetic,
      more potential: inexact state of matter.

In lemonade
      we are all children
      night before first day of school,
      bubbles of pop suspended
      in the crease between
      navel & groin. Beads of sweat
      drizzle our shins; salty glaze
      glues hair to the jut of bone
      behind our ears.

Grape is the sweetest betrayal.
      There is no removing the stain
      of it *say moms everywhere* &
      even if kids choose it last,
      they choose it, as loyal
      to its sugar as any.

Kids will make a game of anything.
This game is to endure the taste
like their cold daily showers:
fingertips aching for each Fahrenheit
in a rush to be done with it all.

Their heads are still too big to assemble
any goal of reason beyond pleasure.
Their eyes are still too big for their heads;
but big enough to collect the mystery of the
pavilion of believers suddenly barely believing.

[Redacted] Earns His Wings

8 March 1978

> *I admire spunk, but not spunk used for*
> *anarchy. Not spunk used against—for rebellion …*
> *you gonna go in the box … That box'll either make*
> *you or break you.*
>
> Community Meeting
> TAPE Q743

The girls slink low in the swings, knees teepeed, and rock.
They braid their arms with the chains as others lean in,
compare notes: Where had he been for the last two days?
And did they see the bubblegum pink ringed by yellow crust
on his elbow where the scab peeled? His hair was so low
his ears looked chilly. Sallow waves no longer poured
into his eyes when he spun upside down on the jungle gym
even though he wasn't good at flips so he was always dangling
scabs he had earned and picked to chase the girls to retreat. His eyes
were moons orbiting his nose ringed with halos distant, deep as
pits in his face. Pink map of rivers crisscrossed the whites.
Five days it took for him to turn peach to grey. He said it
was like standing on one leg, with your eyes closed. Said
after one day of not eating, his stomach forgot and offered
not a whimper of protest. Said his mouth was no longer slick;
he was hollow now and sure enough he dripped from the jungle gym
light as zero gravity.

Imagine, First, a Girl

13 April 1978

A girl tangled between
waking & sleep
gurgles Tower of Power.

Morning registers the
chant; yields her hands
rheumatic

over unlined paper
tanned by sun & age.
She picks at equations

with the point of her pencil
the way she examined
a bug carcass under

her loft. Too noble
for the lowly aspiration
of curiosity, lead parcels

the chore of knowing
to handy tools: dreams,
tanned unlined paper.

As for Dancing
4 July 1978

—thank you;
Thank you for fullness & hunger & sharing them like the dress
I borrowed from Tawanda; for the day off tomorrow; Afro sheen,
spider lashes, his printed salute, at ease, in white jeans
& every lyric the Emotions belted just before the lights came on;

& for the letter from home that said, *I miss you,* & then,
I'm waiting for the bus; for knowing waiting ain't where it's at;
for here: the old folks & the children; the black & white; the beautiful birds
I still duck because I saw *The Birds* & there are no phone booths here;

for taro on my toes & the work of want; for knowing how to do both;
peanut butter fudge—sometimes—& tic-tac-toe with Tawanda, beating
her & laughing long after we should still be laughing because it disturbs
the others; & for Earth, Wind & Fire; because there is nothing better
than a horn section's fingertips twisting my hips under a night sky's
strobes.

After the Game

16 November 1978

Leggy & long-haired,
the boys high-fived through
the entire ride. Peeled

thighs from vinyl for fast
action recaps of every shot,
steal, block & breakaway

while coaches dozed like death
but didn't let up the next day
except lunch: chicken, rice,

an orange apiece for each
hero, hotshot & every play
to make it to the big time.

Looking the Camera in the Eye
17 November 1978

Swell of flesh fat between his eyebrows
skin gathers taut in its corners
skinnying his eyes to slivers
until he has none at all.

His teeth are gentle squares, Chiclets,
less than white from wear, peek at
the congressman and his posse.
In emperor's clothes,
extravagant tales
of wills hexed
jumbee.

Were there sun or a flash
his will would be known.

They all deny they crave salt, dry toes,
relief of dreams. He is no different,
captured midsway to the brass,
bongos and her voice balm
bittersweet as
its petition.

His mystery is glossy wet ink
in the button hole of pupil
that wears particulars
loose; faded over
days in the sun.

Warren Fetus

18 November 1978

For you I am supping
on my tongue; minced
sweet & succulent food
for flies. For you I let
this porch gorge on our
craving, glutton for our
froth & sweat; weak with
the weight of our ask.
For you I empty
the gourd of my black,
poor body: toll, dare,
& legacy. For you I
milked blood through
my breasts; suckled
your breaths; chewed
your tongue & fed it to
the chasers. For you
I dared. Courageous risk,
cloud & clay: You. For you
I am supping on my tongue;
eager & shrinking.

Part 4

What is in the marrow is hard to take out of the bone.
Irish proverb

House on Stilts
18 November 1978

> *The prerequisite for ... judgment is the*
> *available information on which one would exercise*
> *... judgment. And our people were deprived of that.*
>
> *Walter Rodney*
> "JONESTOWN: A CARIBBEAN/
> GUYANESE PERSPECTIVE"

Inventing itself wiser than nature.
Knock-kneed with hand on hip,
a porch for watching the world
pass by without letting the world
watch itself be watched. Punctured
screen plays its part in the clumsy
mission. Architect of lazy cunning
could do better. But wit & panache
trick the eye every time.

A Medic Mistakes Me for Dead

19 November 1978

Belly-up lungs pinch under my swelling;
rictus paints the joke across my face.

I arrived in jellies and jeans;
trunk of socks, *The Red Book*, Prell.

I arrived bared to bone by a by and by
that was supposed to supplant the *X*
of my grandma's signature. Arrived
an allegiance to every girl who stays girl
between Have and Don't and long after
menses. I came brown as the lick of any sun
either side of the equator and unblinking.
I came thirsty impatient for rain and prepared
to memorize the clouds. I came to see
more than my shoes, but I never did.
And even in swelling my flesh still grips my bones.

My cells mobilize to my body's civil war.
Collect around every part of me; I'm one
big wound. Yet the medic does not notice
the stealth gathering; sun licking my sweat
from its lips; all my systems actively not dead.

I am not dead
because I want to be

I am not dead
I want to be

not dead

I am
I want

not dead
to be

am not

because

Sepia

20 November 1978

A reddish-brown color associated particularly with monochrome
photographs of the nineteeth & early twentieth centuries; also
a brown pigment prepared from a black fluid secreted
by cuttlefish used in monochrome. About monochrome:
the term from the ancient Greek *monochromes*
meaning having one color.

Varying tones like your skin a series of subtly shifting browns
secreted from the supposed black of ancestors to cotton
fields. Rows of brown & white coalesce to monochrome
a series of agains blaring through a loudspeaker
again you pout through again
coil into a cocoon of sleep.

In the morning they repeat that your sister is among the rows
of dead which you hear like one might call the frequency
of sepia were it a sound. Were it the loudspeaker's
lullaby how many times would you have to hear
the same thing before you believed it?

After an NBC Interview I Missed You More

28 February 1980

Last Newport glows before blacking
one's hair, then cheek. The photo curls
into 3 a.m. stinking; tucks into my belly
before I suck the last of the cigarette
to the sting of my fingertips. I cannot
face another jungle.

A croak surges from behind my tonsils
to catalogue: you refusing to stay 8,
rope slapping ground; the others 11 & 14.
Always left the screen door open. Too many
times I forgot clouds aren't a field of snipers; too
many times I tasted Judas wine where it wasn't
on your mom's lips. Vietnam did its number
on me. I could not face another jungle.

First day as a daddy I gambled $50. Took it
straight to your mom. There are other things
I take straight: the hairs on my chain snowing
grey in the bowl of a dingy sink; the rank
of the extra gravy; yesterday's limas in the
kitchen trash. The hesitation of numbers
on my paycheck; a deflated woman's acceptance;
pie. But I cannot face another jungle.

Marrow

18 November 1995

Maybe: skin is not
more than dots & dashes;
pattern naked as August
midnight its cover make
believe. Graceless yet as
insistent as absolutes. A
body's largest organ so
unremarkable;
fragile & superfluous.

Mary was appointed to give birth to what would become the world's greatest villain or its savior. Naming is a dubious vocation. He was a boy then teen of average build; nothing in his appearance to suggest eminence. And if he had appetite for distinction, it never showed. He was curious and playful; aged into a mostly simple young man, piecing together furniture, hanging sometimes with his friends, never a girl; a student of potential he evaded tangentially. Potential that offended the populace when he announced it. Potential they punished. With disdain then death. Mary mourned her son. Jews, the son of God. War, grace, famine, feast collected in his name. Naming is a dubious affair. How does a womb resolve the curse of its miracle? Coddling and rearranging the universe the way it does? Maybe it doesn't know. Maybe I didn't either.

—Oil Drum

Acknowledgments

Grateful acknowledgment is made to the Jonestown Institute, especially Fielding McGehee and Rebecca Moore, who supported and championed this work in its earliest and crudest iterations; to Bridgewater Poetry Festival, The Bridge Progressive Arts Initiative, and Annmarie Lockhart for believing, too, in those developing lines; to the Vermont Studio Center and Virginia Center for the Creative Arts for a soft place to land; to the College English Association and Virginia Commission for the Arts for their patronage; to the *Callaloo* Writing Workshops for helping me find my way to and through this work; to Barbara Paterson for her careful and caring red pen; to my dear ancestors Tiffany Austin and Aunt Sarah, for all the times you believed, even when I didn't, that I could; and as always, whatever gods may be. Finally, I am thankful to those who homed early drafts of these poems.

"Making Soap" first appeared in *About Place Journal.*

"I Learn to Love the Body She Loves" and "Jubilee" (under the title "Sunday Open House") first appeared in *Connotation Press.*

"Algebra" and "How Today Will Look When It's History" first appeared in *ITCH.*

The poems "After the Game," "A Revolutionary Love Story," "As for Dancing," "Bookish Girl Sweeps the Sanctuary," "Bucket Brigade," "Composting," "Harvesting," "How Sleep Finds Us," "Wild Child," "Makeshift Daddy," "What We Talk About in Our Cottage," and "Wishing Tree" first appeared in various issues of *jonestown report* from 2010–2018 (some under different titles).

"Disappearance" and an earlier poem that evolved into "Making Soap" ("Grandmother Magic, 13 August 1977") first appeared in *Scratching against the Fabric: Poems from the Bridgewater International Poetry Festival 2013*, edited by Stan Galloway and Timothy Wisniewski (Unbound Content, 2015).

Notes

Shelby County, Alabama, refers to the hometown of Catherine "Hyacinth" Edwards Thrash. In her memoir, *The Onliest One Alive*, she says of her home: "It was equal nothing. 'Stay in your place' was all . . . We'd say, 'Papa, isn't there a better place we can move to?' He'd say, 'We've got our farm here, and it's warm.' You know, old folks was like grounded in the place. You couldn't pull them up. But in 1918 or 1919 we packed up our clothes and bedclothes and caught the train in Wilsonville for Indianapolis."

The Invitation borrows text from the 1965 and 1972 articles of incorporation of the church that became Peoples Temple. "Wings of Deliverance" survived as the name of the church's corporate entity.

The Black Book refers to the way Jim Jones described the Bible. He contended that the Bible had been used to oppress the ancestors of many Peoples Temple parishioners. The poem's epigraph excerpts Dr. Martin Luther King Jr.'s April 1960 appearance on *Meet the Press*.

Water borrows lyrics from "I'm on My Way," a traditional spiritual used as a 1960s antiwar ode, and refers to Odetta, a folk singer who lent her voice to the Civil Rights Movement and recorded the song.

Wild Child portrays the foster and truant children of whom Peoples Temple was awarded custody. While some chose the Temple in lieu of juvenile detention, many were, in essence, kidnapped.

Making Soap portrays one of the projects in which Peoples Temple promised to build a "relationship of friendship and mutual support" with Guyana. There was no soap manufacturer in the country, so all soap had to be imported. Peoples Temple attempted to capitalize on the deficiency by developing a product and brand to be sold in the country.

How Today Will Look When It's History references Steven Bantu Biko (18 December 1946–18 September 1977), a South African anti-apartheid activist and student leader of the burgeoning Black Consciousness Movement in South Africa. He was killed in police custody.

Christine is about Christine Miller. She is the only person recorded expressing dissent to Jim Jones's mandate in the moments before the ordered suicides begin. A native of Texas, Miller had worked her way from picking cotton there to becoming a county clerk in Los Angeles. Peoples Temple members were typically discouraged from retaining "worldly" trappings, but Christine, known for her generosity, was allowed to retain some of her furs and jewelry.

Bucket Brigade describes the Learning Crew, a disciplinary method in which Peoples Temple members were compelled to perform strenuous manual labor to "reeducate" them to the Temple's socialist mission.

Harvesting borrows text from a journal entry of Peoples Temple member Edith Roller. In the entry she discusses the death of Lela Murphy, whose body had to be exhumed after being buried too close to the community's water supply.

Government Name alludes to a practice that made identifying some of the deceased difficult. Some members of Peoples Temple changed their names to signal their commitment to the cause. The practice divorced them from their former lives and signaled their commitment to the community's socialist principles.

When Shanda Said No is about Shanda James Oliver, nineteen, a member of Peoples Temple in whom Jim Jones was sexually interested. When she refused to comply with his advances, she was drugged with the powerful antipsychotic Thorazine and placed in the Extended Care Unit (ECU), where she existed in a semicatatonic state. This was a punishment reserved for potential dissenters and perceived deviants. Shanda was punished several months before the mass deaths and would remain semicatatonic until her death with other members of the community in November 1978.

For Just Pennies a Glass draws its epigraph from the website of Flavor Aid's parent company, Jel Sert. Flavor Aid refers to the powdered drink mix used to concoct the cyanide-laced punch that led to the deaths in Jonestown.

[Redacted] Earns His Wings refers to a disciplinary tactic used in Jonestown. "The box" was a six-foot-by-four-foot underground chamber in which offenders would be confined for varying periods of time.

Looking the Camera in the Eye refers to the celebratory event held hours before the mass deaths on the evening of November 17, 1978.

House on Stilts considers the practice of building homes in Guyana on "stilts" to create a space to escape the tropical heat. The poem excerpts Guyanese scholar-activist Walter Rodney's description of perceived Guyanese indifference to the tragedy at Jonestown in a speech he delivered at Stanford University in 1979.

Sepia references Catherine "Hyacinth" Edwards Thrash and her sister Zipporah "Zip" Thrash, longstanding members of Peoples Temple. Hyacinth survived the events of November 18, 1978, because she refused to go to the pavilion when summoned. Frustrated with Jones's increasingly paranoid rants, she returned to bed, where she was found two days later by members of the National Guard. Her sister was among the dead.

THE UNIVERSITY PRESS OF KENTUCKY
NEW POETRY AND PROSE SERIES

This series features books of contemporary poetry and fiction that exhibit a profound attention to language, strong imagination, formal inventiveness, and awareness of one's literary roots.

SERIES EDITOR: Lisa Williams

ADVISORY BOARD: Camille Dungy, Rebecca Morgan Frank, Silas House, Davis McCombs, and Roger Reeves

Sponsored by Centre College